T0360310

THE
Life-Size
GUIDE
TO THE
NEW ZEALAND
BEACH

featuring the odd things which
get washed up on the sand

Andrew Crowe

PENGUIN BOOKS

Pebbles from Fire Rock

These pebbles have all been worn down from lumps of the world's first rocks (fire rock). Much of this fire rock (or igneous rock) comes from the very hot sticky mixture (**magma**) inside the earth. When this magma cools down *slowly* underground, it forms big crystals (and is known as **plutonic** rock). Melted fire rock (**lava**) erupting from volcanoes cools down much more quickly and is fine-grained, sometimes glassy. (It is this kind of fire rock which is known as **volcanic** rock.)

The main areas to find fire rock.

Mafic ▶

Because they have very little **silica** in them (and lots of iron and magnesium), these pebbles are dark and very heavy. (**Basalt** – below – is also a kind of mafic rock.)

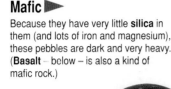

Agate ▲

This is often found in holes in volcanic rock. It looks like wax or smoky glass and is fine-grained, often with dark colour bands. It is popular for making jewellery. Common in Northland, Coromandel Peninsula and Banks Peninsula.

Obsidian / Matā ▲

This looks like black bottle glass but comes from inside a volcano. By knocking chips off with another stone, Māori could use this kind of stone for making razor-sharp cutting tools. Obsidian is washed down from the Central North Island and is found on some beaches of the Bay of Plenty, Mayor Island and Coromandel Peninsula.

Basalt / Karā ▲

Dark, fine-grained rock from inside a volcano. Hard and very heavy. This is one of the commonest rocks on the Earth (and also on the moon). It is very common in Northland, Auckland, around Banks Peninsula, Ōamaru and Dunedin.

Granite

This has cooled slowly and turned solid underground, away from the air. It has big crystals, is hard, tough and speckled with the colours of different minerals (see page 4). Common along Golden Bay, the South Island West Coast and Stewart Island.

• *With orange iron staining*

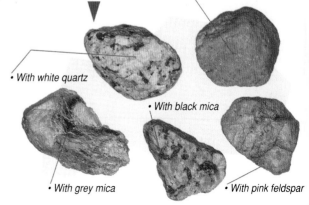

• *With white quartz*

• *With black mica*

• *With grey mica*

• *With pink feldspar*

Pumice / Tāhoata

When melted **rhyolite** rock is blown out of a volcano, it comes out like a thick, sticky milkshake. When the volcano blows, explosions of hot gas throw out frothy lumps which can be carried thousands of kilometres by the wind. Because pumice is full of steam-holes, it will often float on water. Indeed, some pieces found on north-east Northland beaches have floated here all the way from Tonga!

Central North Island Volcanic Rock

The main white part of the rock is probably **rhyolite**. The black block-like bits in it look like lumps of charcoal but are really crystals of a mineral called **pyroxene**. Found around Northland, Auckland, Coromandel Peninsula and Taranaki.

Unless otherwise indicated, all photos are shown at life-size

Pebbles from Layered Rock

[Sedimentary Rock]

This kind of rock is usually softer than other kinds. Over time, rain, wind and waves wear down the older rocks to make rock dust and sand. This dust settles in layers on the bottom of lakes and seas. It is buried and squashed deep underground for millions of years, pressing the dust hard until it makes this layered rock. Sandwich layers of this kind of rock are common in coastal cliffs, where they have often been folded and tilted. Animals and plants buried in these layers millions of years ago may leave clear impressions or remains (**fossils**).

The main areas to find layered rock.

Conglomerate Rock ▶

The pebbles inside this rock have been rolled and rounded by ocean waves or washed down rivers. They have then been re-cemented together to form new rock. This lump of concrete-like rock has in turn been rolled again and worn smooth by the sea to form a new pebble. Sometimes called **puddingstone**.

• Pebbles within pebbles

• Fossilised remains of snail-like seashell (gastropod)

◀ Sandstone with Fossils

Sandstone is made from squashed sand. Creatures buried in the sand can leave impressions or remains like this from millions of years ago. These two pieces contain the fossils of shellfish.

• Fossilised remains of hinged seashell (bivalve)

Limestone / Pākeho ▶

Made from ground-up shells of shellfish and coral, etc. This fine dust and sand has then been pressed and cemented together underground.

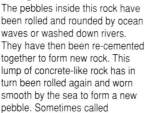

Chert

This glass-like rock can be white, grey, black, yellowish, red, orange or green. Impressions in it are often left by sponges and very small sea animals. Chert is found on some Northland and Coromandel beaches, also near Auckland and Dunedin. ◀

Mudstone ▶

Mudstone is made from squashed mud. The holes in this piece have been made by a kind of shellfish. The shellfish uses the rough surface of its shells to grind back and forth, slowly boring a tunnel in which to hide. Mudstone is common and so are these holes in it.

Sandstone ▶

(from fire rock)

Note the red and green colouring. The original fire rock was worn down to make sand and pebbles which were later pressed together and heated to make sandstone.

• Streaks of quartz

Greywacke ▲

A kind of very hard, light grey sandstone, often with hard dark grey to black mudstone layers in it. Common in the South Island and near Wellington. Breaks easily.

◀ Limonite

Some of the iron found in black sand dissolves. This rusty water then soaks through soft sandstone to make these rounded lumps. Common in Northland, West Auckland and Golden Bay.

Unless otherwise indicated, all photos are shown at life-size

3

Pebbles from Pressure-Cooked Rock

[Metamorphic Rock]

This third kind of rock is made from other rocks which have been changed by heat or very high pressure (or both). It has been so deeply buried and squashed by the weight of rock above it that it gets layered like a sandwich. This kind of rock tends to glisten in the light, often looks streaky and breaks open into thin layers, rather like the pages of a book. More common in the South Island.

The main areas to find pressure-cooked rock.

Greenstone / Pounamu

A tough streaky rock, usually (but not always) green. Also known as **nephrite jade**. Used by Māori for making tools and jewellery. Found mostly along the West Coast of the South Island, especially just north of Hokitika. Pieces found on the beach often have a greasy-looking surface. (Boulders of greenstone can have a thick grey, whitish or yellowish-green crust, making them look just like common rocks.)

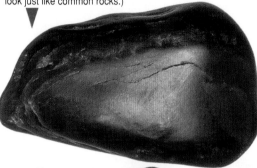

• *The brick-coloured bits are iron staining*

Glittering Meta-Sandstones

Pressure-cooked **sandstone** (see page 3), mostly from the South Island. The white flaky bits are a kind of mineral called **muscovite mica** which splits into paper-thin layers. It is called muscovite because it was used for window panes in Moscow.

• *Stained orange with iron*

• *These layers have been folded*

• *The white sandwich layers are **quartz** and **feldspar***

• *Broken schist*

Schist

This slate-like rock is made from pressure-cooked **mudstone** and **sandstone** (see page 3). It breaks easily into flat flakes so is useful for making stone walls and simple roof tiles. Common on some South Island beaches.

Marble

Made from pressure-cooked **limestone** (see page 3). So soft that you can scratch it with a knife. Used for making polished sculptures. Mostly from the South Island.

Pebbles from Minerals

Rocks are made from a mix of hundreds of minerals. The individual pieces of pure mineral are often too small to be seen without a magnifying glass or microscope. Sometimes, however, these minerals are found in pure lumps (as shown here). Other less common minerals include **pyroxene** (page 2), **garnet** (page 5) and **mica** (above).

Feldspar

This splits into flat blocks. Often pinkish, sometimes cream or white. Particularly common near Karamea on the West Coast of the South Island. One of the world's most common minerals.

Quartz / Kiripaka

Often clear and glassy, it is made up of six-sided crystals. Sometimes tinted with other colours. It is hard enough to scratch glass and cannot be scratched with a knife. Used in glass-making and jewellery. Common in Northland, Coromandel Peninsula, Taranaki and Banks Peninsula, near Ōamaru, Greymouth and Invercargill. One of the world's most common minerals.

Unless otherwise indicated, all photos are shown at life-size

Sand / Onepū

Sand is made mostly from broken rocks being washed down to the sea by the larger local rivers. You may also find green pieces among the grains from the broken spines of urchins, blue from mussel shells and pink from deep water barnacles (see below). Try looking at sand through a microscope. (Up to 50x magnification.) Even under a magnifying glass, it can look quite stunning – like a heap of precious jewels.

Crunchy Golden Sand ▲

From the Golden Bay area of the South Island. This coarse crunchy sand is made from **granite** (see page 2) which has been stained with iron oxide. As the grains are ground up more finely by the sea, the golden staining is washed off to make creamy-grey sand.

Light Grey Sand ▲

Common around the lower North Island and along the north and east coast of the South Island. This sample is from Tahuna Beach, Nelson and is from **greywacke** and **schist** rock (see pages 3 & 4).

Pumice Sand / Tātāhoata ▲

This sand is so lightweight that it drifts along the beach with even the softest breath of wind. Toss a handful of it into the air to test it. Common in the Bay of Plenty. This sample is from Mahia Peninsula.

Shelly Sand ▲

From Otama Beach on the Coromandel Peninsula, this sand is made up of shells which have been ground up by the sea.

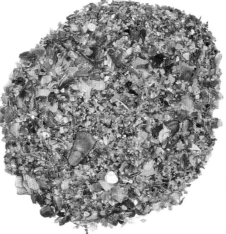

Pink Shelly Sand ▲

Like most pink sand, this comes from the shells of **large pink barnacles** (see page 16). This sample is from Hot Water Beach on the Coromandel Peninsula.

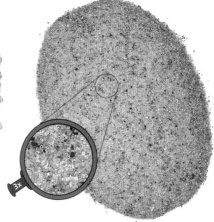

Squeaky White Sand ▲

Very fine, silky sand from Otama Beach on the Coromandel Peninsula. When dry, it squeaks underfoot when you scuff your feet. It is almost pure silica from **quartz**-rich rock. This sand can be so white that, on a bright sunny day, it is painful to look directly at it without sunglasses.

Black Iron Sand ▲

This heavy black sand comes from Karioitahi (near Port Waikato) and has been washed northward from the Taranaki volcanoes. On such rough surf beaches, the lighter **quartz** sand (paler and less heavy) is swept away by the ocean currents. Iron sand sticks to a magnet. Patches of it can be almost purple. In the middle of summer, dry iron sand can get so hot that you can't even walk on it with bare feet.

Sparkling Pink Sand ▲

This unusual pink sand is from Woodpecker Bay, between Greymouth and Westport. The colouring is from a group of minerals called **garnet**. Larger pieces are washed down many Westland rivers and are common along this stretch of coast.

Powdery White Sand ▲

This sand from Pakuranga Beach (Auckland) is as fine as talcum powder or chalk. It comes from a very soft white rock called **ignimbrite** ('fire shower rock' made from volcanic ash welded together by heat). This ash came whooshing from the Taupo area at about 1000 kph, arriving in Auckland about 15 minutes later!

Tracks (& Other Signs)

Many signs of life on the beach are found in the sand. Small holes in wet sand may be from the breathing tubes of **hinged shellfish** (like pipi), from **bristleworms** (page 22) or **shrimps** (page 16). Larger holes may be from **small crabs** (page 14) or **sand-burrowing sea cucumbers**. A mound of dry sand next to a burrow is often a sign of **sandhoppers** (page 16). Footprints tell us about the shyer beach animals and animals of the night, showing which way the animal was going, how fast and even what it was doing along the way. Around piles of seaweed, for example, you'll see which birds feed on the beetles and sandhoppers found there. Early morning is the best time to look, or shortly after rain has washed old tracks away. By clearing and smoothing an area regularly you can create a 'track bed' to find out which animals visit, how often and when. The tracks of many animals are best recognised by the trail pattern rather than the footprint itself. But for the tracker, the first step is to learn the difference between the footprint of a:

- **BIRD** (Note that ducks, shags and seabirds all have webbed feet.)
- **2-TOED ANIMAL** (with the 'split hoof' of a **deer**, **cow**, **sheep**, **goat** or **pig**. A **horse** leaves a single hoof print).
- **4-TOED ANIMAL** (a **dog** or **cat**, or the prints from the *front* feet of a **rat** or **mouse**).
- **5-TOED ANIMAL** (a **person**, **possum**, **hedgehog**, **ferret**, **stoat** or **weasel**, or the prints from the *back* feet of a **rat** or **mouse**).

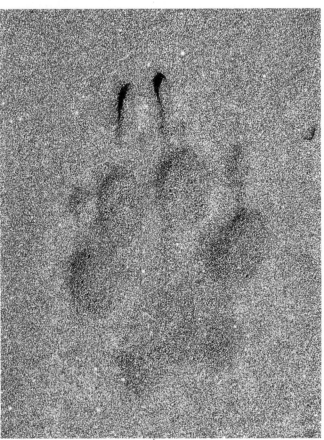

Footprint of a Large Dog

Four toes. Note that the claws show clearly on the footprints of a dog but NOT on the footprints of a **cat**. (Because a cat can withdraw its claws.)

Cast of a Marine Worm

Several kinds of native **bristleworms** live in the wet sand, swallowing sand to digest any food attached to the sand grains. When the tide is out, squiggly lines like these can be seen. These piles are made from the sand after it's been through the worm.

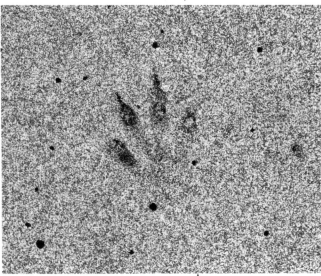

Footprint of a Hedgehog

These have long toes (claws). The print of the fifth toe can often be hard to see. These introduced pests search the beach at night for birds' eggs and insects, and their footprints are common on many beaches. *Sometimes* a hedgehog's spines drag in the sand and leave a trail but often they don't.

Droppings of a Black-Backed Gull

The most common droppings on many beaches are from dogs (sorry: no photo). But the prize for the most beautiful must go to these droppings from a black-backed gull which has recently enjoyed a meal of **violet snails** (page 18). Gull vomit is also common on the beach, showing that these birds will try to swallow the strangest things (including broken glass).

Unless otherwise indicated, all photos are shown at life-size

Footprints of a Banded Dotterel ▲

Common on some beaches. Note that the toes of a dotterel are not webbed. The pattern of prints from the rarer New Zealand dotterel look the same, only slightly larger.

Footprint of a Pūkeko

Very long hind toe. This is the largest bird footprint you are likely to find on a New Zealand beach. Note that a pūkeko's feet are even larger than those of a heron.

Footprint of an Oystercatcher ▲

Common on many beaches. Note that the toes have no webbing between them and that they often leave very deep prints like this.

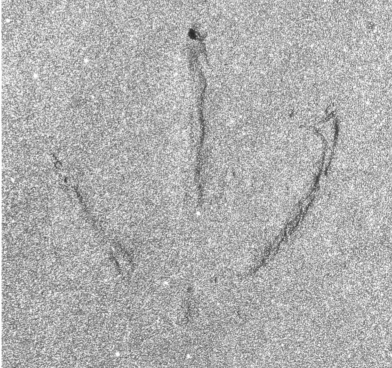

Footprint of a Black-Backed Gull ▲

One of the most common footprints on the beach. (The footprint of the **red-billed gull** is similar but smaller.) Although all gulls have webbing between their toes, this doesn't always leave a clear impression on the sand.

Unless otherwise indicated, all photos are shown at life-size

Sea & Farm Animals (Bones & Teeth)

On this page are the hard remains of warm-blooded animals like us which give milk to their young. Some of these are from introduced farm animals (like **sheep**). Others are from native marine mammals like **whales**, **dolphins** and **seals**. Among these marine mammals are the true giants of the deep, the largest of which (the **blue whale**) can be as long as three city buses parked end to end.

◀ Tooth of a Common Dolphin
Dolphins have lots of little teeth on both jaws. (The whole dolphin can be up to 2.3 metres long.)

◀ Tooth of a Fur Seal
This is one of the two longest front teeth from the seal's lower jaw. (The body length of an adult male fur seal can be up to 1.8 metres.)

• *Fur seal* (not life-size!)

▲ Ear Bone of a Large Whale
A separate bone from inside the ear of a large whale (possibly a **sperm whale**). Such fluid-filled bones from the ears of seals or whales are stronger than any of their other bones, so are often the only part to survive. (Our own ear bones are no bigger than our little fingernail.)

◀ Tooth of a Large Whale
The *really* large whales (like the **blue whale**) don't have teeth like this. They have 'baleen plates' which work like tea-strainers, sieving out fine particles of food from the sea water. So the tooth shown here may be from a **sperm whale** (which can be up to 18 metres long or longer than one and a half city buses).

Ambergris / Tūtae-Tohoraha from a Sperm Whale ▶
Strong-smelling, gummy, coffee-coloured lumps like this are ambergris from the intestines of a **sperm whale**. Ambergris has a sweet smell, like pipe tobacco and is collected for making certain kinds of perfume. The whale is thought to use this to help it digest the tough beaks of squid.

Skull of a Possum ▶
The remains of dead possums are common on many beaches.

◀ Backbone of a Farm Animal
This is one of the backbones (vertebra) of a farm animal. It could be from a young cow.

Jaw of a Sheep ▶
The bones and teeth of dead sheep are often washed down streams and up onto the beach. Their teeth are often badly worn like this from chewing grass all day.

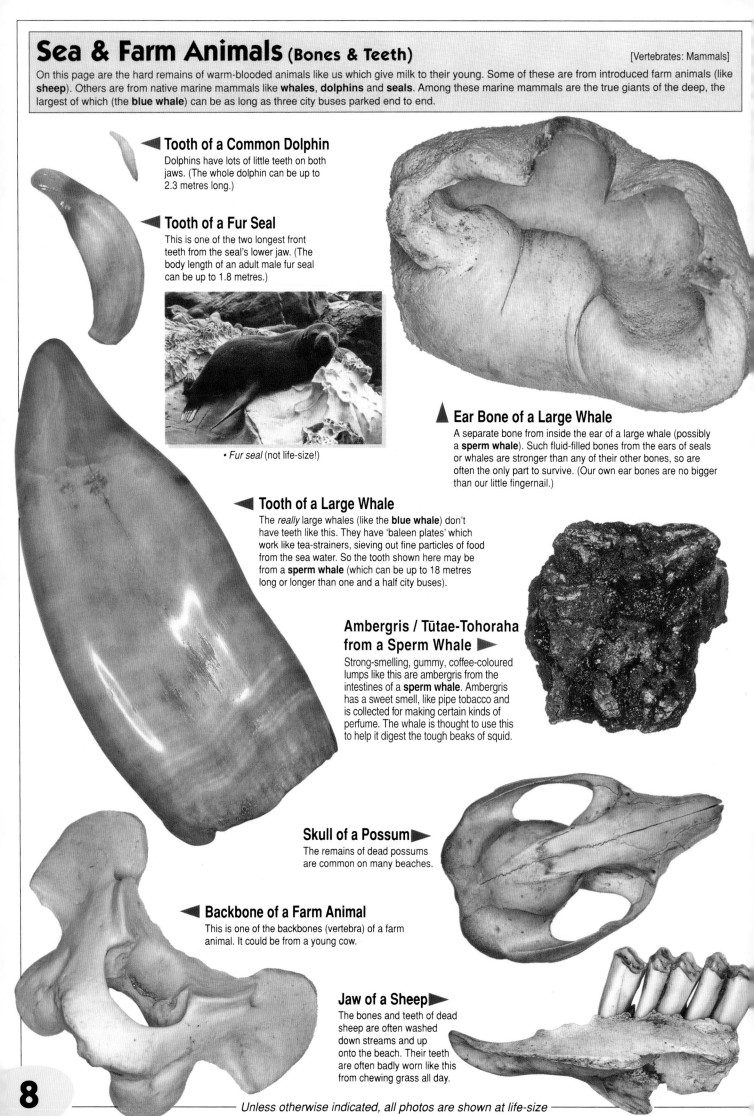

Unless otherwise indicated, all photos are shown at life-size

Bird / Manu (Bones & Feathers)

[Vertebrates: Aves]

The remains of birds are common along the drift-line on the beach. Clean bones can usually be recognised as coming from birds because they are so lightweight. The bones of gulls and shags are particularly common but over 100 kinds of seabirds (mostly **albatrosses**, **petrels**, **prions** and **shearwaters**) are found around New Zealand. The remains of many of them can be recognised from their bills alone. For a start (unlike other birds) these ocean birds are all 'tubenoses', which means that you will see a pair of large tubes (nostrils) on top of their bill. The skull of our largest seabird (**wandering albatross**) can be so large, it wouldn't even fit on this page.

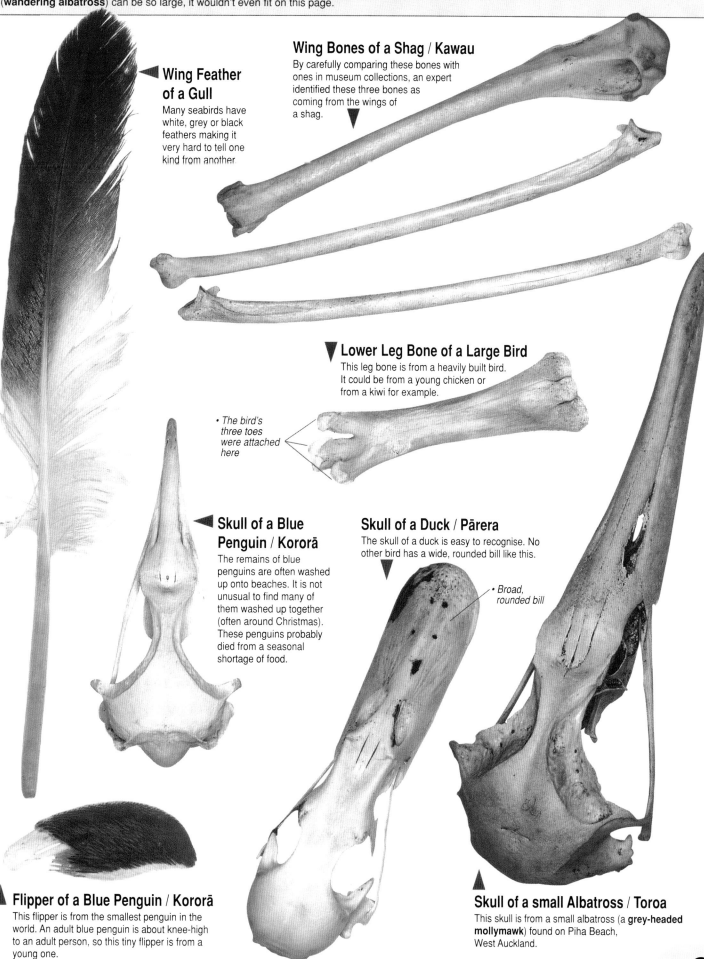

Wing Feather of a Gull

Many seabirds have white, grey or black feathers making it very hard to tell one kind from another.

Wing Bones of a Shag / Kawau

By carefully comparing these bones with ones in museum collections, an expert identified these three bones as coming from the wings of a shag.

Lower Leg Bone of a Large Bird

This leg bone is from a heavily built bird. It could be from a young chicken or from a kiwi for example.

• The bird's three toes were attached here

Skull of a Blue Penguin / Korora

The remains of blue penguins are often washed up onto beaches. It is not unusual to find many of them washed up together (often around Christmas). These penguins probably died from a seasonal shortage of food.

Skull of a Duck / Pārera

The skull of a duck is easy to recognise. No other bird has a wide, rounded bill like this.

• Broad, rounded bill

Flipper of a Blue Penguin / Korora

This flipper is from the smallest penguin in the world. An adult blue penguin is about knee-high to an adult person, so this tiny flipper is from a young one.

Skull of a small Albatross / Toroa

This skull is from a small albatross (a **grey-headed mollymawk**) found on Piha Beach, West Auckland.

The bony remains of fish are often found tangled among the seaweed on the drift-line. This page shows a selection of the more puzzling fishy things beachcombers are likely to find.

• Has spines like a porcupine

▶ Porcupine Fish / Kōpūtōtara

Allomycterus jaculiferus
The remains of this odd-looking fish are often washed up around the North Island. When alive, a porcupine fish scares off other fish by swallowing water to puff up its body. It also has a nasty bite, has poisonous spines and is poisonous to eat. A big one can be as long as 60cm. Long after the porcupine fish has died, its **swim bladder** (from inside the fish) is often all that remains (see photo).

• Porcupine fish swim bladder

▶ Seahorse / Manaia

Hippocampus abdominalis
This magical-looking fish lives among seaweed on rocks in sheltered harbours all around New Zealand. It sucks up tiny creatures in the water while using its curled tail to hold onto the seaweed. The female lays her eggs in the male's tummy pouch for him to look after. With the tail uncurled, a big seahorse can be as much as 25cm long (almost the height of this page).

• The living seahorse uses its tail to hold onto seaweed (not life-size)

◀ Tail Barbs of Stingray / Hoto

Dasyatis species
These barbs (hoto) are from the animal's stinging tail. Divers can swim right up to a stingray (whai or oru) without harm, but if you are unlucky enough to stand on one, it will lash out with its tail, using these barbs to leave a deep and very painful wound. (When angry with a diver, the stingray raises its tail as a warning.) A large stingray can be two metres or more across.

• Supraorbital ridge (eye bone) of a snapper

Teeth of a small Shark / Mangō

[Selachiformes]
Unlike humans, sharks have several rows of teeth. As sharks eat nothing but meat, these teeth are very sharp for cutting through and tearing the flesh of other large animals.

• Otolith (ear bone) of a snapper

▲ Jawbone of a Fish

The teeth and jawbones of fish are commonly found.

▲ Odd Bones of a Snapper / Tāmure

Chrysophrys auratus
Beachcombers finding these odd-looking bones are often puzzled. The larger bone comes from above the eye of a snapper and is called a **supraorbital ridge**. The other small one is called an **otolith**. When the rest of the snapper has rotted away, this little bone from inside the fish's ear is often all that remains. Fishes use these little bones for hearing and for balance. By cutting an otolith and examining its growth rings, experts can tell the fish's age and can tell one kind of fish from another.

◀ Backbone of a Fish

The vertebra (backbone) of a bony fish.

Unless otherwise indicated, all photos are shown at life-size

Sea Urchins / Kina

[Echinoderms: Echinoidea]

At first, it might seem odd that scientists group sea urchins together with starfish. But note how the shell of a sea urchin is divided into a five-part star-like shape – rather like the arms of a starfish. The name 'urchin' means 'hedgehog' for the common urchin does look rather like a hedgehog. Between their stiff, movable spines, urchins have flexible tube-feet with suckers on the end to get a good grip on rocks and seaweed. Sea urchins eat mostly seaweed (but also sponges and sea anemones) and have free-swimming larvae (young). There are about 20 different kinds living around the New Zealand coastline, all of them native to New Zealand. Here are the more common ones.

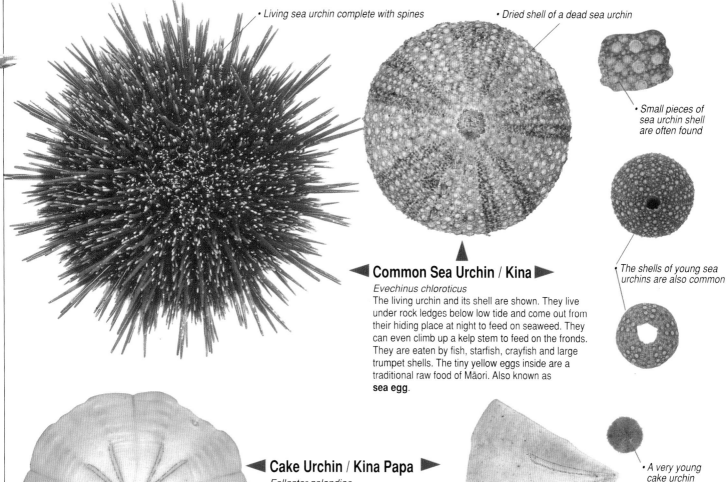

• Living sea urchin complete with spines

• Dried shell of a dead sea urchin

• Small pieces of sea urchin shell are often found

• The shells of young sea urchins are also common

◀ Common Sea Urchin / Kina ▶

Evechinus chloroticus
The living urchin and its shell are shown. They live under rock ledges below low tide and come out from their hiding place at night to feed on seaweed. They can even climb up a kelp stem to feed on the fronds. They are eaten by fish, starfish, crayfish and large trumpet shells. The tiny yellow eggs inside are a traditional raw food of Māori. Also known as **sea egg**.

◀ Cake Urchin / Kina Papa ▶

Fellaster zelandiae
These flat shells feel rough like sandpaper. Children often skim them across the waves. When living, this shell is covered with short, fine brown spines. The animal uses these for digging itself just under the surface of fine sand, at or below low tide. It gets eaten by snapper. Also called **sand dollar**, **snapper biscuit** or **dollar biscuit**.

• A very young cake urchin

• The complete dried shell of a cake urchin (after the hair-like spines have washed off)

• The inside of old cake urchin shells has an interesting pattern of reinforcing

• Old shells break neatly into five cake-like slices. (Each slice can then be opened like a sandwich cake to reveal interesting patterns – left – which can be used in collage artwork)

• Shell, heart-shaped

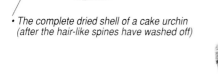

◀ Heart Urchin / Kina Pakira

Echinocardium australe
The living animal looks rather like a mouse with no tail. It spends its life buried in the sand, using its hair-like spines to move. By the time it is washed ashore, the spines have usually been washed off to leave this fragile heart-shaped shell.

Kina Poka

Apatopygus recens
The shell of this is similar to that of the heart urchin but smaller, flatter and much stronger. Another clear difference is an oval hole on top, off-centre in a shallow groove. Found on Northland beaches but is not common. A very similar one (*Echinobrissus recens*) is sometimes washed up on Nelson beaches and on Stewart Island.

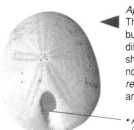

• An oval hole on top sits off-centre in a small groove

Unless otherwise indicated, all photos are shown at life-size

11

Starfish / Pātangaroa

[Echinoderms: Asteroidea & Ophiuroidea]

Although most people call these animals 'starfish', many scientists prefer to call them **sea stars** [Asteroidea] and **brittle stars** [Ophiuroidea]. Although these creatures don't have eyes and can't see, they can still use the tips of their arms to sense dark and light. Some lay eggs; others give birth to live young. When eating small animals (especially shellfish) and tiny seaweeds, sea stars often push their stomach out through their own mouth (which is underneath). The food is digested outside the body and then drawn back in again. The faster-moving brittle stars collect tiny particles of food by combing the water with their arms. (They are called 'brittle stars' because their arms break off so easily.) In all, there are about 150 known kinds of sea star in New Zealand waters and over 165 brittle stars, all of them native to New Zealand. Here is a selection of the more common ones.

• Arms shorter than width of central disk

• Main arms longer than width of central disk

• Two damaged arms are regrowing

▲ Reef Star / Pātangaroa

Stichaster australis [Asteroidea]

A large sea star with 10 to 12 arms. It has a tough grey skin, tinged with blue and orange. The odd one can be as bright as a tangerine. Found clinging to surf-lashed rocks along the west coast of both the North and South Islands. They can suck open mussels and crush whole sea urchins. Unless you surprise them, they are almost impossible to pull off the rocks. Also called the **surf starfish**. Can be up to 35cm across.

◄ Spiny Star / Papatangaroa

Coscinasterias calamaria [Asteroidea]

Common along most of the New Zealand coastline. Because it has up to 11 slender prickly arms, this large sea star is also known as the **eleven-armed starfish**. Young ones are green to blue-grey, but turn dull orange with age. They eat all kinds of shellfish (particularly oysters and pipi) which they suck open with their many little tube feet. Can be up to 35cm across.

Unless otherwise indicated, all photos are shown at life-size

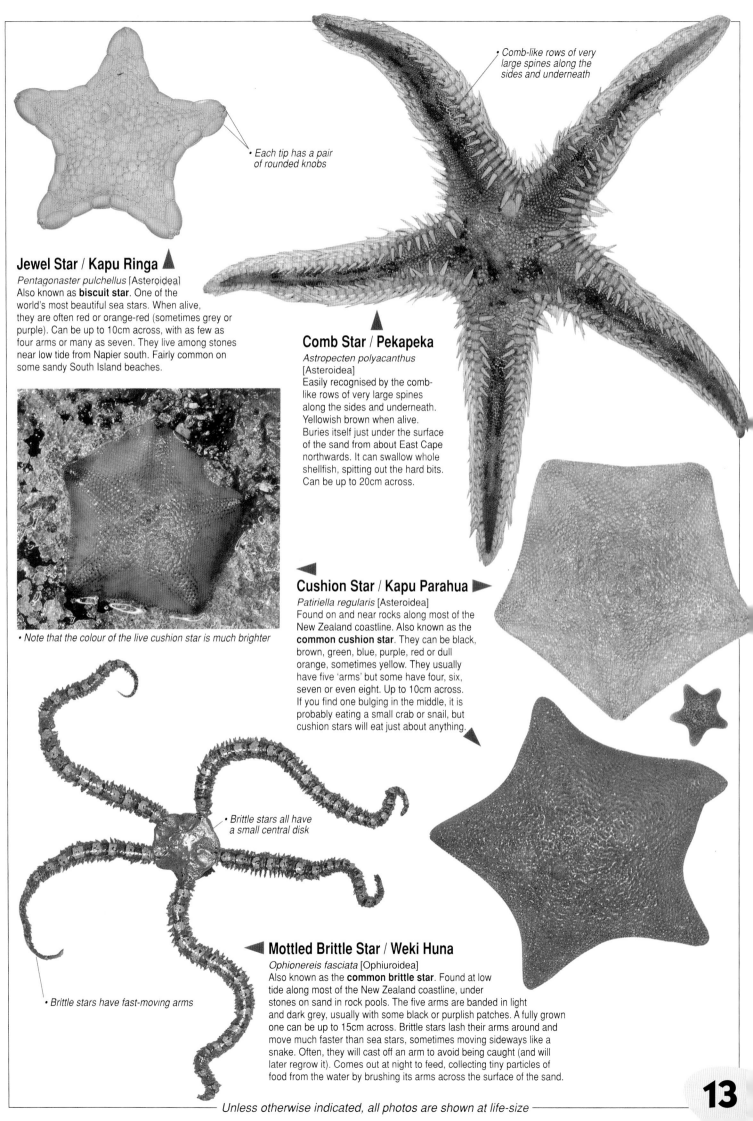

• Each tip has a pair of rounded knobs

• Comb-like rows of very large spines along the sides and underneath

Jewel Star / Kapu Ringa ▲

Pentagonaster pulchellus [Asteroidea]
Also known as **biscuit star**. One of the
world's most beautiful sea stars. When alive,
they are often red or orange-red (sometimes grey or
purple). Can be up to 10cm across, with as few as
four arms or many as seven. They live among stones
near low tide from Napier south. Fairly common on
some sandy South Island beaches.

• Note that the colour of the live cushion star is much brighter

Comb Star / Pekapeka

Astropecten polyacanthus
[Asteroidea]
Easily recognised by the comb-
like rows of very large spines
along the sides and underneath.
Yellowish brown when alive.
Buries itself just under the surface
of the sand from about East Cape
northwards. It can swallow whole
shellfish, spitting out the hard bits.
Can be up to 20cm across.

◀ Cushion Star / Kapu Parahua ▶

Patiriella regularis [Asteroidea]
Found on and near rocks along most of the
New Zealand coastline. Also known as the
common cushion star. They can be black,
brown, green, blue, purple, red or dull
orange, sometimes yellow. They usually
have five 'arms' but some have four, six,
seven or even eight. Up to 10cm across.
If you find one bulging in the middle, it is
probably eating a small crab or snail, but
cushion stars will eat just about anything.

• Brittle stars all have a small central disk

• Brittle stars have fast-moving arms

◀ Mottled Brittle Star / Weki Huna

Ophionereis fasciata [Ophiuroidea]
Also known as the **common brittle star**. Found at low
tide along most of the New Zealand coastline, under
stones on sand in rock pools. The five arms are banded in light
and dark grey, usually with some black or purplish patches. A fully grown
one can be up to 15cm across. Brittle stars lash their arms around and
move much faster than sea stars, sometimes moving sideways like a
snake. Often, they will cast off an arm to avoid being caught (and will
later regrow it). Comes out at night to feed, collecting tiny particles of
food from the water by brushing its arms across the surface of the sand.

13

Crabs & Crayfish / Pāpaka me Kōura

[Crustaceans]

Most crabs have very flat bodies, allowing them to squeeze into narrow cracks between rocks and to hide under boulders. Crabs breathe water but can survive for several hours in air so long as they keep their gills wet. They have eyes on the end of stalks. Most will eat almost anything. If a crab loses a claw, it can usually grow a new one. Male crabs have bigger claws. As both crabs and crayfish grow too big for their hard shell-like skin, they climb out of the old skin, rather like pulling a hand out of a glove, and the new skin underneath begins to harden. These old skins and claws are often washed up on the beach along with whole dead crabs. So far, almost 200 kinds of crab have been found in New Zealand waters and 3 kinds of saltwater crayfish.

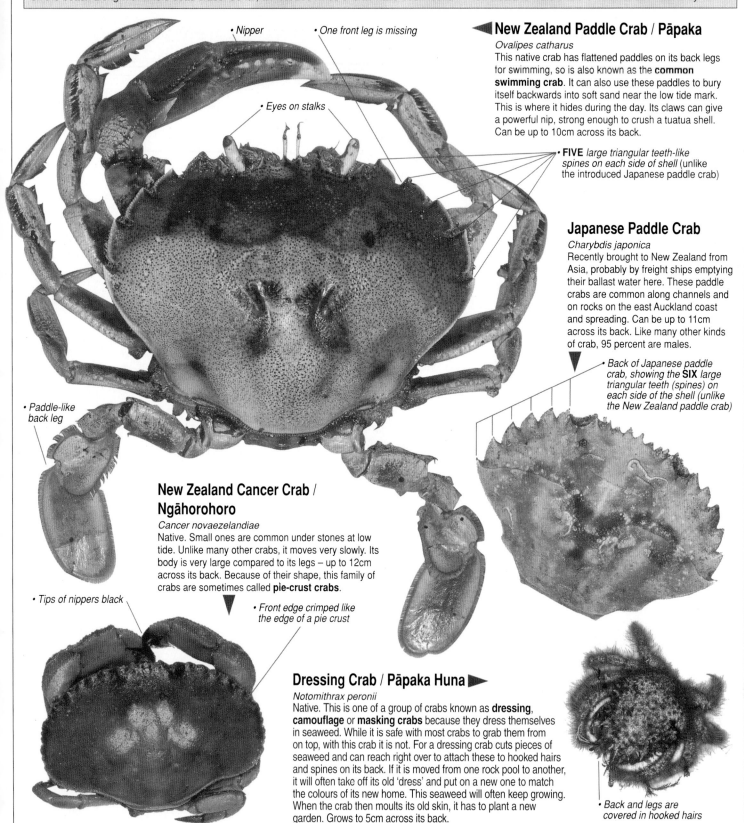

• Nipper

• One front leg is missing

• Eyes on stalks

• Paddle-like back leg

• Tips of nippers black

New Zealand Paddle Crab / Pāpaka

Ovalipes catharus
This native crab has flattened paddles on its back legs for swimming, so is also known as the **common swimming crab**. It can also use these paddles to bury itself backwards into soft sand near the low tide mark. This is where it hides during the day. Its claws can give a powerful nip, strong enough to crush a tuatua shell. Can be up to 10cm across its back.

• **FIVE** large triangular teeth-like spines on each side of shell (unlike the introduced Japanese paddle crab)

Japanese Paddle Crab

Charybdis japonica
Recently brought to New Zealand from Asia, probably by freight ships emptying their ballast water here. These paddle crabs are common along channels and on rocks on the east Auckland coast and spreading. Can be up to 11cm across its back. Like many other kinds of crab, 95 percent are males.

• Back of Japanese paddle crab, showing the **SIX** large triangular teeth (spines) on each side of the shell (unlike the New Zealand paddle crab)

New Zealand Cancer Crab / Ngāhorohoro

Cancer novaezelandiae
Native. Small ones are common under stones at low tide. Unlike many other crabs, it moves very slowly. Its body is very large compared to its legs – up to 12cm across its back. Because of their shape, this family of crabs are sometimes called **pie-crust crabs**.

• Front edge crimped like the edge of a pie crust

Dressing Crab / Pāpaka Huna ▶

Notomithrax peronii
Native. This is one of a group of crabs known as **dressing**, **camouflage** or **masking crabs** because they dress themselves in seaweed. While it is safe with most crabs to grab them from on top, with this crab it is not. For a dressing crab cuts pieces of seaweed and can reach right over to attach these to hooked hairs and spines on its back. If it is moved from one rock pool to another, it will often take off its old 'dress' and put on a new one to match the colours of its new home. This seaweed will often keep growing. When the crab then moults its old skin, it has to plant a new garden. Grows to 5cm across its back.

• Back and legs are covered in hooked hairs

Hairy Crab / Pāpaka Huruhuru

Pilumnus species
Native. These live under stones, in rock pools or in rock crevices. When disturbed, they freeze. The whole crab is covered with matted hairs which trap silt. This camouflage makes them very hard to see. Can be up to 18mm across its back.

• Tips of nippers almost black

Mud Crab / Kairau

Helice crassa
Native. Very common on mudflats where it lives in burrows or under stones. It prefers to keep the same burrow and will defend this if necessary. It is most active when the tide is out. Can be up to 2cm across its back. Also known as the **tunnelling mud crab**, **square-back** or **short-eyed mud crab**.

• Square back

14

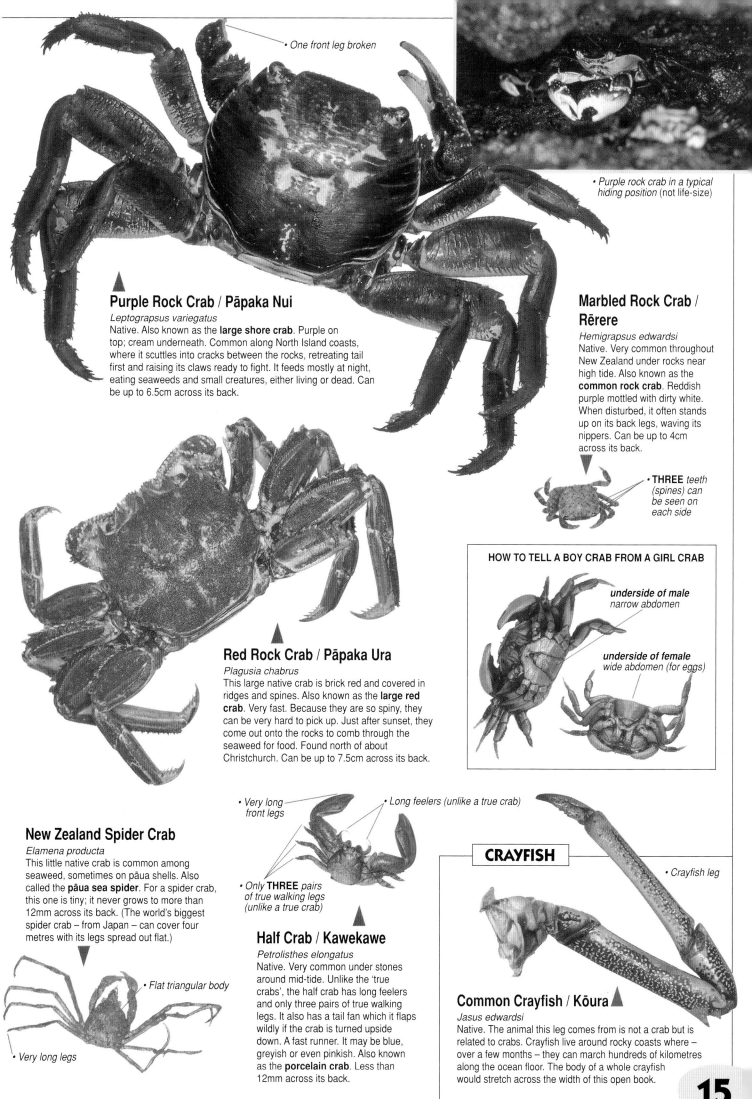

• One front leg broken

• Purple rock crab in a typical hiding position (not life-size)

Purple Rock Crab / Pāpaka Nui

Leptograpsus variegatus
Native. Also known as the **large shore crab**. Purple on top; cream underneath. Common along North Island coasts, where it scuttles into cracks between the rocks, retreating tail first and raising its claws ready to fight. It feeds mostly at night, eating seaweeds and small creatures, either living or dead. Can be up to 6.5cm across its back.

Marbled Rock Crab / Rērere

Hemigrapsus edwardsi
Native. Very common throughout New Zealand under rocks near high tide. Also known as the **common rock crab**. Reddish purple mottled with dirty white. When disturbed, it often stands up on its back legs, waving its nippers. Can be up to 4cm across its back.

• **THREE** teeth (spines) can be seen on each side

HOW TO TELL A BOY CRAB FROM A GIRL CRAB

underside of male narrow abdomen

underside of female wide abdomen (for eggs)

Red Rock Crab / Pāpaka Ura

Plagusia chabrus
This large native crab is brick red and covered in ridges and spines. Also known as the **large red crab**. Very fast. Because they are so spiny, they can be very hard to pick up. Just after sunset, they come out onto the rocks to comb through the seaweed for food. Found north of about Christchurch. Can be up to 7.5cm across its back.

New Zealand Spider Crab

Elamena producta
This little native crab is common among seaweed, sometimes on pāua shells. Also called the **pāua sea spider**. For a spider crab, this one is tiny; it never grows to more than 12mm across its back. (The world's biggest spider crab – from Japan – can cover four metres with its legs spread out flat.)

• Flat triangular body

• Very long legs

• Very long front legs

• Long feelers (unlike a true crab)

• Only **THREE** pairs of true walking legs (unlike a true crab)

Half Crab / Kawekawe

Petrolisthes elongatus
Native. Very common under stones around mid-tide. Unlike the 'true crabs', the half crab has long feelers and only three pairs of true walking legs. It also has a tail fan which it flaps wildly if the crab is turned upside down. A fast runner. It may be blue, greyish or even pinkish. Also known as the **porcelain crab**. Less than 12mm across its back.

CRAYFISH

• Crayfish leg

Common Crayfish / Kōura

Jasus edwardsi
Native. The animal this leg comes from is not a crab but is related to crabs. Crayfish live around rocky coasts where – over a few months – they can march hundreds of kilometres along the ocean floor. The body of a whole crayfish would stretch across the width of this open book.

Unless otherwise indicated, all photos are shown at life-size

◀ Modest Barnacles / Tio Piripiri

Austrominius modestus (was *Elminius*)
The white star-shaped barnacles on this mussel shell commonly appear between the tides on shellfish, stones, boats and driftwood. Also known as the **common small barnacle**. The animal which lives inside feeds by reaching out with its feathery legs, combing through the water for tiny bits of food.

• Hundreds of goose barnacles attached to a piece of driftwood (not life-size)

Large Pink Barnacles / Tiotio ▶

Notomegabalanus decorus
These are found around most of the New Zealand coastline, often attached to other shells. However, the living barnacle is rarely seen as it usually lives about 25 metres under the sea. Shown here are three barnacles, two of them attached to the shell of a siphon whelk. In many places, the sand is made pink with pieces of the broken barnacle shells (see page 5).

Goose Barnacles / Werewere ▲

Lepas anatifera
This looks like a shellfish on the end of a worm-like stalk. It is usually attached to driftwood. Found worldwide, it often gets washed up on west coast beaches. How did the goose barnacle get its name? Many centuries ago, people in England believed that a kind of goose hatched out from the white shells. Much of the driftwood the barnacles are attached to has been washed off (or thrown off) Japanese fishing boats.

Skins of Common Shrimps / Tarawera

Palaemon affinis
The living animal is common in and around rock pools. They can walk or swim, and eat dead plants and animals. When they grow, they have to shed their skin and grow a new one.

• One of the feathery feeding legs

• Nippers normally attached here

• Stalked eyes

Mantis Shrimps / Mana ▶

Lysiosquilla spinosa
This shrimp hides in a vertical tunnel (up to one metre deep) in mud or sandflats near the low tide mark. Its body is so flexible that it can do a U-turn inside its tunnel. Its oversized nippers give it the look of a praying mantis. (By the time the shrimp is washed up, these hooked, crab-like nippers have often broken off.) It can also swim.

• Some goose barnacle stems are very long (up to 20cm long)

• Much smaller goose barnacles are common on **ram's horn shells** (see page 18)

Sandhopper / Potipoti

Talorchestia quoyana [Amphipoda] ▶
These jumping, flea-like creatures eat rotting fish and seaweed. Some people even call them **beach fleas** (but they are not related to true fleas). During the day, they burrow into damp sand, often hiding underneath piles of seaweed. Look out for little heaps of dry sand on top of wet sand. This is often where a group of them have buried a piece of seaweed. Pick sandhoppers up and they tickle your hand as they try to bury themselves between your fingers. They can survive long periods underwater. New Zealand has about 12 different kinds.

▼ Beach Slater / Pāpapa

[Isopoda]
These are native cousins of the common garden slater. They can sometimes be seen running quickly over the beach. When they stop suddenly, they seem to disappear. This is because they are speckled with exactly the same colours as the sand they live on. If they spot movement, they can also curl up into a tiny ball. They are easiest to see if you keep very still and approach them slowly with a magnifying glass. Beach slaters feed on just about anything they find. There are many different kinds.

16

Insects & Spiders

Of the insects and spiders which are found on the coast, some live only here, by the sea. In rock pools, for example, you may find the native **saltpool mosquito** (near high tide) or **marine spider** (near mid-tide, often underwater!). Behind the beach, in the dunes, you may come across long **orange sand centipedes** running over the sand or little black **native bees** disappearing into tiny tunnels. Flying among the dunes are **spider-hunting wasps**, **Chinese paper wasps** and the large hovering **Convolvulus hawk moths**. But the main insects and spiders of the beach itself are all shown below.

Common Copper Butterfly / Pepe Para Riki

Lycaena salustius complex
A common native butterfly seen in mid-summer around sand dunes. Flies fast and jerkily. Its little green slug-like caterpillars eat the leaves of the native pōhuehue vine.

Large Sand Scarab / Mumutawa ▶

Pericoptus truncatus
During the day, this large native beetle buries itself deep in the sand. At night, it leaves clear tracks in the sand or flies about noisily (in spring). The grubs live under logs, eating rotten driftwood and dead grass roots.

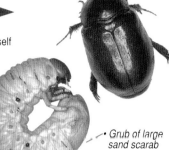

• *Grub of large sand scarab*

Large Coastal Rove Beetle

Cafius litoreus
Native. Common just above high water mark, feeding on the **kelp fly** maggots found in decaying seaweed. Can fly.

Seaweed Darkling Beetle ▶

Chaerodes trachyscelides
Native. Common under seaweed or driftwood. Flightless. If you lift the seaweed, they quickly bury themselves in the sand. Try picking up a handful of the beetles. Feel how they tickle as they try to bury themselves between your fingers.

Dark Patch Lax Beetle ▲

Thelyphassa diaphana
A very common native beetle under driftwood along the shoreline. They use a poisonous chemical to defend themselves, so take care. You can get blisters just from touching them.

◀ Sand Dune Tiger Beetles

Cicindela perhispida
(was *Neocicindela*)
Native. Fast runners. Come near them and they often fly just out of reach. They come in various colours according to the colour of the local sand.

Hairy Kelp Fly

Chaetocoelopa littoralis
Native. Seen around rotting seaweed where the maggots feed. Using their long, hairy legs, the adult fly can walk on water. (There are other bigger kelp fly species in the South Island.)

Beach Stiletto Fly ▶

Megathereva bilineata
(was *Anabarrhynchus*)
Native. Seen on the beach in summer. The long, cream or pink maggots burrow in the sand, hunting other small creatures.

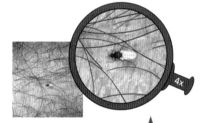

Biting Midge / Naonao ▲

Styloconops myersi
Native. Smaller than a sand fly, but its **bite** can be more painful and irritating. Found on beaches around Nelson, Bay of Plenty, North Cape and the Coromandel.

Sand Fly / Namu ▲

Austrosimulium species
Native. Found throughout New Zealand, particularly in warm weather. During the day, the females bite. (The males don't bite.)

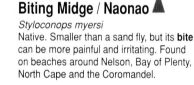

SPIDERS

Bumble Bee / Pī Rorohū

Bombus species
These fat, furry bees often get blown into the sea and are washed up alive on the edge of the incoming tide.

Poisonous female

◀ Katipo Spider / Katipō

Latrodectus katipo
Native. Lives mostly in the dunes behind beaches but is not common. The adult female has a poisonous bite. The male is much smaller and doesn't bite. But don't worry! Even the female katipō is not that dangerous, for no one has died from its bite over the past one hundred years.

Honey Bee / Pī Honi ▶

Apis mellifera
These often get blown into the sea and are seen struggling along the edge of the incoming tide. Take care. It is easy to step on one and get stung.

◀ Seashore Earwig / Matā

Anisolabis littorea
Native. Common above high-tide on pebble beaches, hiding under stones and driftwood, near seaweed and other plants. (There is also an **introduced seashore earwig** which has wings and is not so darkly coloured.)

Seashore Wolf Spider ▶

Anoteropsis litoralis [Lycosidae]
Native. One of several similar speckled grey spiders which live on beaches and sand dunes. They don't build webs to catch their prey, but run fast to hunt for their food – which is why they are called wolf spiders. This one is seen around the North Island and Canterbury, and can be different colours depending on the sand it lives in. The adults are more active at night; young ones during the day.

For creatures with more than 8 legs, go to **hoppers**, **slaters**, etc., opposite.

17

— *Unless otherwise indicated, all photos are shown at life-size*

There are enough different kinds of shells on the beach to fill a whole book (see **Useful Books** on the inside back cover). Indeed, New Zealand has over 2500 different kinds (if you count all the really tiny ones)! Some of the larger ones are such jewels to look at that the beachcomber can hardly help collecting them. Here is a selection of the more beautiful ones.

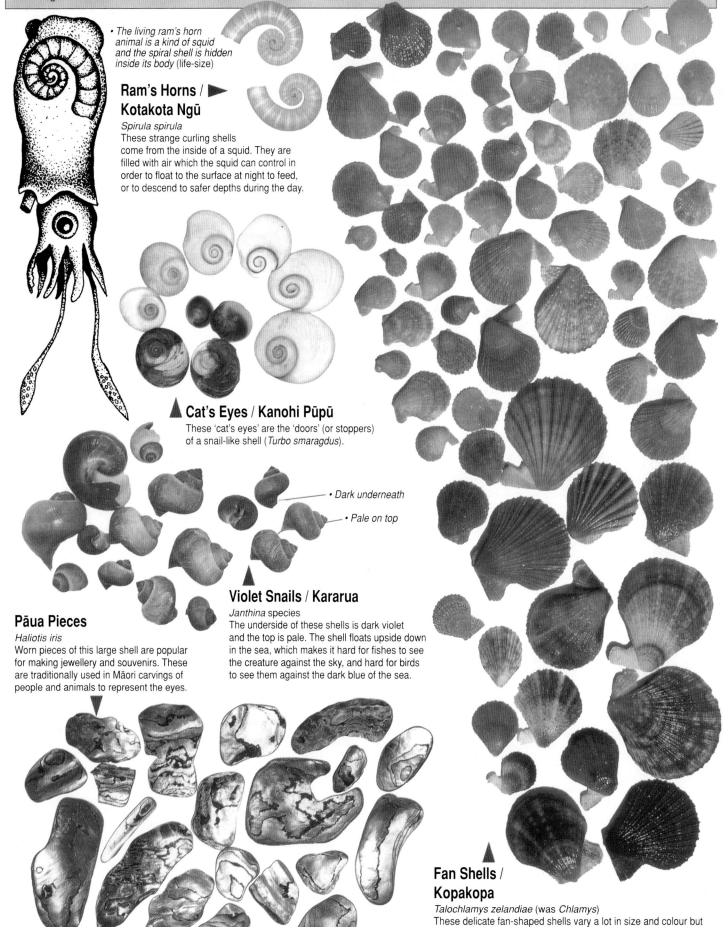

• *The living ram's horn animal is a kind of squid and the spiral shell is hidden inside its body (life-size)*

Ram's Horns / ▶
Kotakota Ngū

Spirula spirula
These strange curling shells come from the inside of a squid. They are filled with air which the squid can control in order to float to the surface at night to feed, or to descend to safer depths during the day.

▲ **Cat's Eyes / Kanohi Pūpū**
These 'cat's eyes' are the 'doors' (or stoppers) of a snail-like shell (*Turbo smaragdus*).

• *Dark underneath*

• *Pale on top*

Pāua Pieces

Haliotis iris
Worn pieces of this large shell are popular for making jewellery and souvenirs. These are traditionally used in Māori carvings of people and animals to represent the eyes.

Violet Snails / Kararua
Janthina species
The underside of these shells is dark violet and the top is pale. The shell floats upside down in the sea, which makes it hard for fishes to see the creature against the sky, and hard for birds to see them against the dark blue of the sea.

Fan Shells /
Kopakopa

Talochlamys zelandiae (was *Chlamys*)
These delicate fan-shaped shells vary a lot in size and colour but are always rough to touch. The commonest shade is orange, but they can also be white, dark grey, yellow, pink, red, reddish-brown or deep purple, sometimes patterned with stripes or blotches. One ear (at the hinge of the shell) is always much larger than the other.

Unless otherwise indicated, all photos are shown at life-size

Eggs (of Fish, Shellfish & Squid)

Eggs of an Elephant Fish / Reperepe
Callorhynchus milii
These large egg capsules are often washed up on beaches along the east coast of the South Island. The little shark-like fish which lays them is not much longer than twice the height of this page and has a snout like a very short elephant's trunk.

Eggs of a Skate / Whai
Raja nasuta
The fish which lays these hard egg-cases looks like a stingray. Skate egg-cases are tied to the ocean floor at each corner by long, coiled tendrils, each case containing just one baby skate. Also known as a **mermaid's purse**.

• Tendrils anchor the egg-case to the ocean floor

Eggs of a Squid / Ngū
[Mollusca: Cephalopoda]
When they are still fresh, strings of these eggs look like clumps of white sausages. They are often washed up still attached to seaweed. You can sometimes see the tiny dark eyes of the squid inside.

Eggs of a Speckled Whelk
Cominella adspersa
Tufts of these egg capsules are often attached to rocks, loose stones, shells and other hard objects (like this mussel shell). These are laid by a smallish brown snail-like shellfish with a speckled shell.

Eggs of a Siphon Whelk
Penion sulcatus
These egg capsules have been laid by a large creamy-white snail-like shellfish. Each capsule has a papery coating. Tiny but fully formed whelks crawl out of these.

Eggs of a White Rock Shell
Dicathais orbita
These clusters of eggs are laid by a large, heavily-ridged snail-like shellfish. These egg clusters feel rather like plastic packaging and are often found on stones and shells and under ledges.

Eggs of a Knobbed Whelk
Austrofusus glans
A knobbly white snail-like shellfish has laid these egg capsules in long rows. Here, long chains of them are attached to a finger sponge.

Eggs of a Volute
Alcithoe arabica
A long smooth scroll-like shellfish has attached this hard egg case to a pipi shell. From it, several small volutes will hatch out.

Eggs of a Nudibranch
[Mollusca: Gastropoda]
Nudibranchs (or **sea slugs**) lay their eggs in spirals like this on rocks. These spirals come in a range of colours which often match the colour of their parents. Each spiral contains many thousands of eggs.

Unless otherwise indicated, all photos are shown at life-size

19

Jellyfish & their Relatives / Kakaru Moana

[Coelenterates]

These animals have no brains but can hunt and defend themselves by using their tentacles to sting. These tentacles are covered in tiny hairs. When the hairs are touched, a hollow thread flicks out into the intruder's skin and the jellyfish injects its poison. Many jellyfish are quite harmless to people, but the sting of the **Portuguese man-o'-war** can be very painful.

Portuguese Man-O'-War / Ihu Moana

Physalia physalis

Hundreds of these can sometimes be found washed up near the high-tide mark after a storm on beaches north of Hokitika. This creature may look like a single animal, but it is really a whole community of tiny organisms (called **hydroids**), each of which has a different job. It has a see-through gas float and streaming blue tentacles which can give a painful burning sting on soft skin. Although the main gas bubble is only 6 – 7cm long, the tentacles can be several metres long and can sting long after the creature has been washed up. It eats fish. It is also known as a **bluebottle** and is not a true jellyfish.

• *Stinging tentacles*

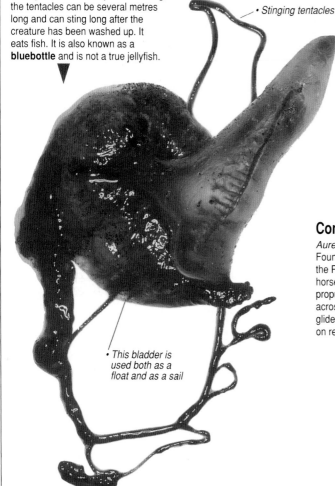

• *This bladder is used both as a float and as a sail*

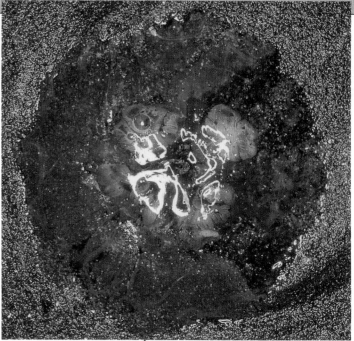

Common Jellyfish / Petipeti ▲

Aurelia aurita

Found throughout the world. Very common here north of Taranaki in spring and summer. Unlike the Portuguese man-o'-war and by-the-wind sailor, this is a single animal. Four bluish purple horseshoe-shaped patches can be seen inside. It uses these to reproduce. Jellyfish swim by jet propulsion, squirting out a jet of water from underneath about every two seconds. If you come across one when you are snorkelling, you'll be surprised how graceful they look, pulsating as they glide slowly by. Unlike some tropical jellyfish, this one is completely harmless to people. It feeds on really tiny plants and animals and can be up to 20cm across (about the size of a dinner plate).

By-The-Wind Sailor / Katiaho Rere ▲

Velella velella

This isn't a true jellyfish but a community of creatures (called **hydroids**), each with a different job. Up to 5cm long. Often washed up along west coast beaches in summer. Although the by-the-wind sailor is harmless to people, it can sting much smaller creatures. In turn, its fringe of very short tentacles are often nibbled by floating **violet snails** (page 18).

Sea Anemone / Kōtore Moana ▲

[Actiniaria]

Several different kinds of sea anemones live in rock pools and on rocks below high tide. They can be yellow, pink, red, purple, blue, green, brown or white. These flower-like animals use their sensitive petal-like tentacles to sting small creatures and pass them down into their mouth. On human skin, these tentacles feel sticky to touch but are quite harmless to people. Some sea anemones can split in half to make two anemones. Many can move slowly from place to place. One – the **wandering sea anemone** – can even release its foot to float around before reattaching itself to the rock.

Unless otherwise indicated, all photos are shown at life-size

Sea Firs & Corals

[More Coelenterates (including Hydrozoa & Anthozoans)]

Sea firs [Hydrozoa] look like miniature plants with roots but are really communities of tiny animals. These and **true corals** [Anthozoa] are both related to sea anemones (but you'll need a magnifying glass to see the similarity).

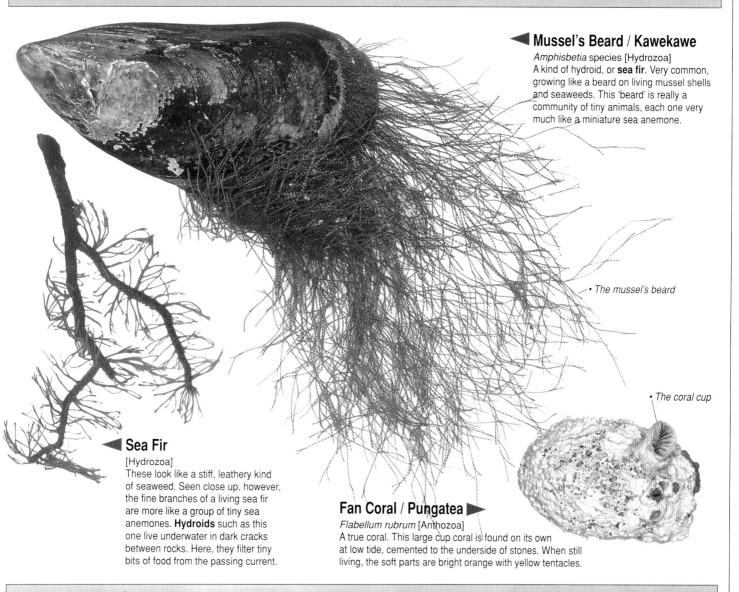

◀ Mussel's Beard / Kawekawe

Amphisbetia species [Hydrozoa]
A kind of hydroid, or **sea fir**. Very common, growing like a beard on living mussel shells and seaweeds. This 'beard' is really a community of tiny animals, each one very much like a miniature sea anemone.

• *The mussel's beard*

• *The coral cup*

◀ Sea Fir

[Hydrozoa]
These look like a stiff, leathery kind of seaweed. Seen close up, however, the fine branches of a living sea fir are more like a group of tiny sea anemones. **Hydroids** such as this one live underwater in dark cracks between rocks. Here, they filter tiny bits of food from the passing current.

Fan Coral / Pungatea ▶

Flabellum rubrum [Anthozoa]
A true coral. This large cup coral is found on its own at low tide, cemented to the underside of stones. When still living, the soft parts are bright orange with yellow tentacles.

Moss Animals

[Bryozoans]

Moss animals [Bryozoa] also live as communities, many of them growing as flat crusts over stones, shells and seaweeds; others are branching. So far, 640 different kinds have been found in New Zealand waters.

• *A different kind of lace coral that's soft and bendy (scientific name unknown)*

Lace Coral / Punga Tatari ▶

Hippelozoon novaezelandiae [Bryozoa]
A Bryozoan or **moss animal** community. These stiff, chalky sea mats form coral-like growths which are often washed up on the beach like tufts of delicately folded lace. Very slow-growing. There are many different kinds, but even the experts have trouble telling one from another.

• *A different kind of lace coral (scientific name unknown)*

• *The true lace coral is stiff (Hippelozoon novaezelandiae)*

Sea Mat (growing on plastic) ▲

[Bryozoa]
Much of what is washed up onto the beach (including pebbles, seaweeds, shells and plastic) is covered with this very fine chalky 'honeycomb'. Each hole in the honeycomb is really a tiny box with a lid. These boxes form a kind of submarine 'apartment block'. Each member of the **moss animal** community lifts the lid of its home to feed.

Unless otherwise indicated, all photos are shown at life-size

Bristleworms

Although **bristleworms** [Polychaeta] are one of the commonest kinds of creatures of the seashore, you don't often hear about them. This group of creatures includes **tubeworms** (which stay at home inside a tube) and **burrowing worms** (which, of course, burrow). Many of these burrowing worms provide food for wading birds such as oystercatchers. So far, 485 different kinds have been found in New Zealand waters.

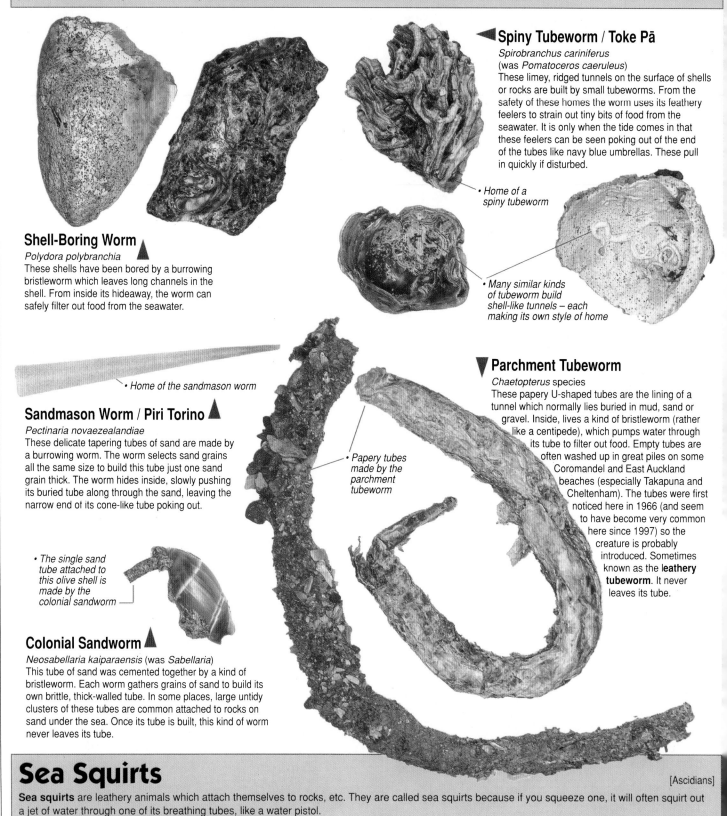

Spiny Tubeworm / Toke Pā

Spirobranchus cariniferus
(was *Pomatoceros caeruleus*)
These limey, ridged tunnels on the surface of shells or rocks are built by small tubeworms. From the safety of these homes the worm uses its feathery feelers to strain out tiny bits of food from the seawater. It is only when the tide comes in that these feelers can be seen poking out of the end of the tubes like navy blue umbrellas. These pull in quickly if disturbed.

• *Home of a spiny tubeworm*

• *Many similar kinds of tubeworm build shell-like tunnels – each making its own style of home*

Shell-Boring Worm

Polydora polybranchia
These shells have been bored by a burrowing bristleworm which leaves long channels in the shell. From inside its hideaway, the worm can safely filter out food from the seawater.

• *Home of the sandmason worm*

Sandmason Worm / Piri Torino

Pectinaria novaezealandiae
These delicate tapering tubes of sand are made by a burrowing worm. The worm selects sand grains all the same size to build this tube just one sand grain thick. The worm hides inside, slowly pushing its buried tube along through the sand, leaving the narrow end of its cone-like tube poking out.

• *The single sand tube attached to this olive shell is made by the colonial sandworm*

Colonial Sandworm

Neosabellaria kaiparaensis (was *Sabellaria*)
This tube of sand was cemented together by a kind of bristleworm. Each worm gathers grains of sand to build its own brittle, thick-walled tube. In some places, large untidy clusters of these tubes are common attached to rocks on sand under the sea. Once its tube is built, this kind of worm never leaves its tube.

Parchment Tubeworm

Chaetopterus species
These papery U-shaped tubes are the lining of a tunnel which normally lies buried in mud, sand or gravel. Inside, lives a kind of bristleworm (rather like a centipede), which pumps water through its tube to filter out food. Empty tubes are often washed up in great piles on some Coromandel and East Auckland beaches (especially Takapuna and Cheltenham). The tubes were first noticed here in 1966 (and seem to have become very common here since 1997) so the creature is probably introduced. Sometimes known as the **leathery tubeworm**. It never leaves its tube.

• *Papery tubes made by the parchment tubeworm*

Sea Squirts

Sea squirts are leathery animals which attach themselves to rocks, etc. They are called sea squirts because if you squeeze one, it will often squirt out a jet of water through one of its breathing tubes, like a water pistol.

Sea Tulip / Kāeo ▶

Boltenia pachydermatina [Ascidiacea]
A stalked **sea squirt** (or Tunicate) common in the South Island, particularly around Oamaru, but smaller ones are sometimes washed up along North Island coasts. Squeeze one and it squirts a jet of water. As its common name suggests, it looks more like a plant than an animal. Big ones can be almost a metre long.

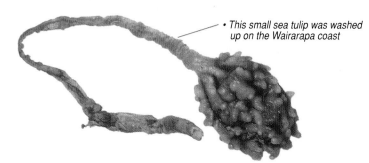

• *This small sea tulip was washed up on the Wairarapa coast*

Unless otherwise indicated, all photos are shown at life-size

Sponges / Kōpūpūtai

[Porifera]

Many sponges look very much like plants, but they are really communities of tiny animals. Whereas true plants need sunlight, sponges can live in the dark, deep inside caves. They draw in water through many tiny holes, filtering out tiny particles of food before pumping the used water out through larger holes. Some sponges have been mashed up and put through a very fine sieve. Within a few hours, this sponge soup has been seen arranging itself into a whole new sponge! Telling one kind of sponge from another can be very difficult, even for the expert. Even so, in New Zealand waters, almost 450 different kinds have so far been found and named.

Finger Sponge / Kōpūpūtai

Callyspongia species

Pieces often wash up after storms, sometimes still attached to a shellfish or piece of rock. There are many different kinds. When alive, finger sponges are yellow to purple but the dead sponges found on beaches have often faded. Their 'fingers' can be short and fat, or thin and up to one metre long. Unlike the branches of seaweeds, these branching sponge fingers often divide then join up again.

Encrusting Sponge

[Porifera]

These sponges grow like a carpet over dark, hidden surfaces under stones and ledges at or below low tide. When living, they can be red, orange, yellow, purple or black. By the time chunks of them are washed up onto the beach, they have usually faded. To tell one species from another even an expert needs a microscope.

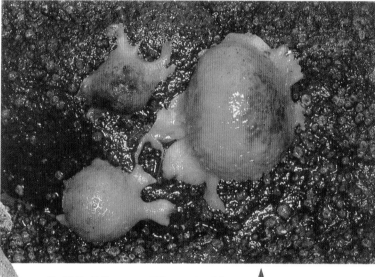

Golf Ball Sponge / Porotaka Moana

Tethya aurantium

This leathery sponge is bright orange like a tangerine skin, so is also known as the **orange golf ball sponge**. It is very common in rock pools all around New Zealand, under boulders and overhangs near low tide. You may have to lie down on the rock to get low enough to spot them. Also called **globe sponge**.

Shell eaten away 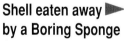 by a Boring Sponge

Cliona celata

A tiny orange sponge has bored into this shell, leaving hundreds of holes. The animal uses acid to dissolve these tunnels as a place in which to hide. From the safety of these holes, it feeds by filtering its food from the seawater.

Seaweed / Rimurimu (Red)

Of the three main colours of seaweed (red, brown and green), these seaweeds are bright red to purple – but often bleach in the sun and rain to white, pink, brown or green. Most of the 600 or more kinds of seaweed around New Zealand are in this group. Many of these seaweeds prefer shade, so these are found only in deeper water. This means that unless they are washed up in a storm, the tide has to be a long way out to see many of them. Most of the red seaweeds shown here are ones which often get washed up onto the beach.

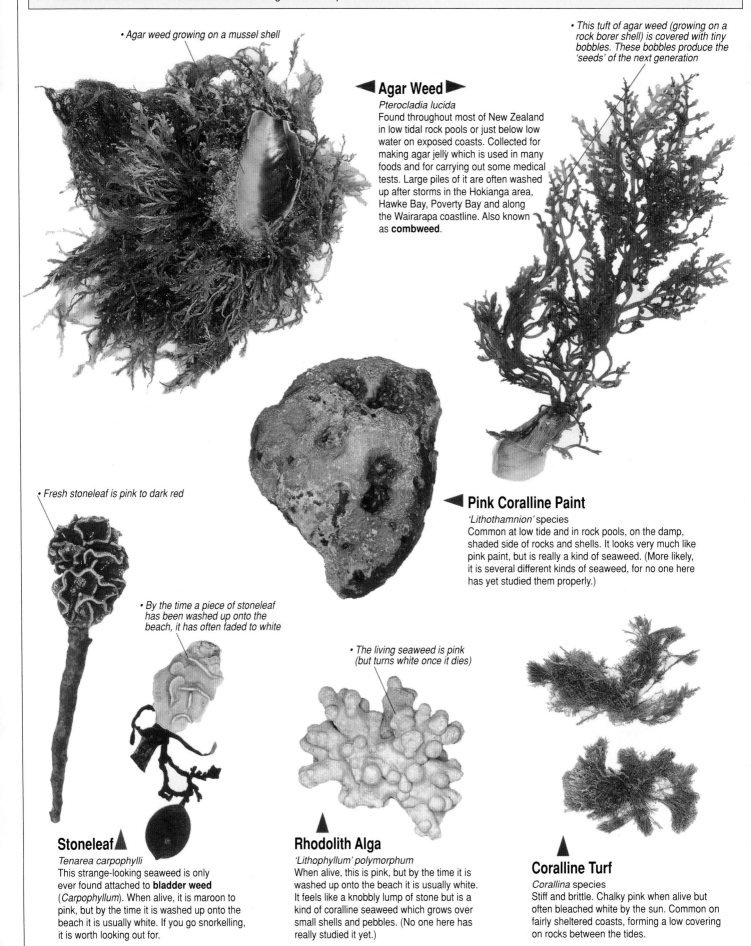

• Agar weed growing on a mussel shell

• This tuft of agar weed (growing on a rock borer shell) is covered with tiny bobbles. These bobbles produce the 'seeds' of the next generation

◀ Agar Weed ▶

Pterocladia lucida
Found throughout most of New Zealand in low tidal rock pools or just below low water on exposed coasts. Collected for making agar jelly which is used in many foods and for carrying out some medical tests. Large piles of it are often washed up after storms in the Hokianga area, Hawke Bay, Poverty Bay and along the Wairarapa coastline. Also known as **combweed**.

• Fresh stoneleaf is pink to dark red

◀ Pink Coralline Paint

'Lithothamnion' species
Common at low tide and in rock pools, on the damp, shaded side of rocks and shells. It looks very much like pink paint, but is really a kind of seaweed. (More likely, it is several different kinds of seaweed, for no one here has yet studied them properly.)

• By the time a piece of stoneleaf has been washed up onto the beach, it has often faded to white

• The living seaweed is pink (but turns white once it dies)

Stoneleaf ▲

Tenarea carpophylli
This strange-looking seaweed is only ever found attached to **bladder weed** (*Carpophyllum*). When alive, it is maroon to pink, but by the time it is washed up onto the beach it is usually white. If you go snorkelling, it is worth looking out for.

Rhodolith Alga ▲

'Lithophyllum' polymorphum
When alive, this is pink, but by the time it is washed up onto the beach it is usually white. It feels like a knobbly lump of stone but is a kind of coralline seaweed which grows over small shells and pebbles. (No one here has really studied it yet.)

Coralline Turf ▲

Corallina species
Stiff and brittle. Chalky pink when alive but often bleached white by the sun. Common on fairly sheltered coasts, forming a low covering on rocks between the tides.

Unless otherwise indicated, all photos are shown at life-size

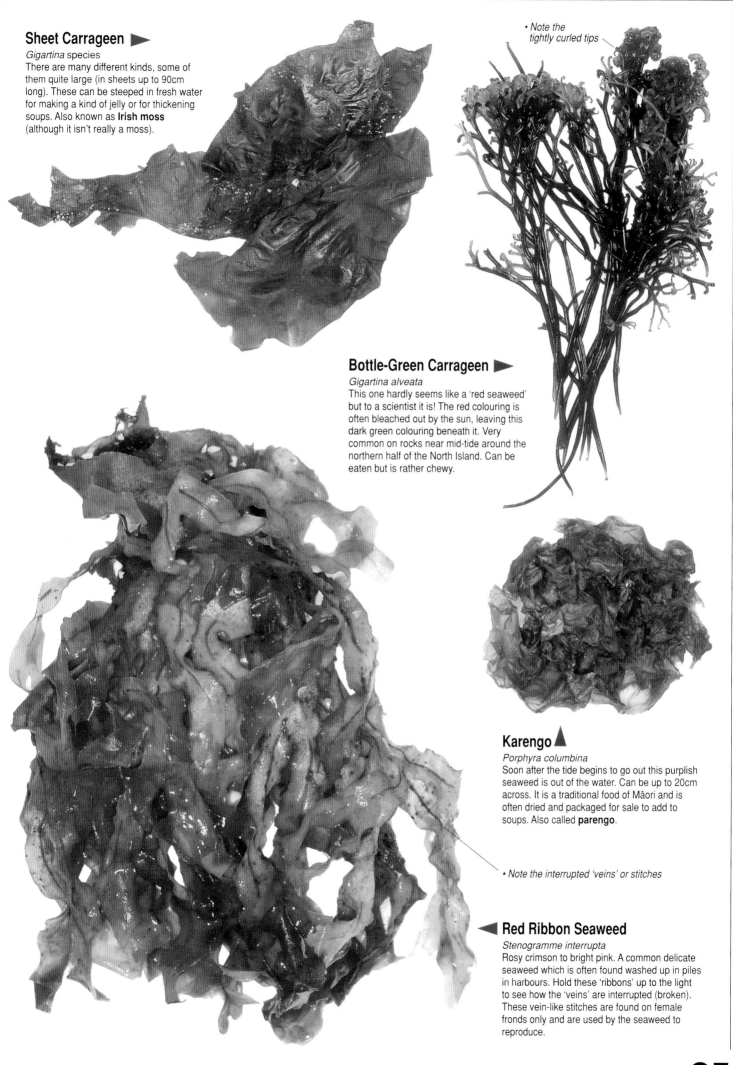

Sheet Carrageen ▶

Gigartina species
There are many different kinds, some of them quite large (in sheets up to 90cm long). These can be steeped in fresh water for making a kind of jelly or for thickening soups. Also known as **Irish moss** (although it isn't really a moss).

• *Note the tightly curled tips*

Bottle-Green Carrageen ▶

Gigartina alveata
This one hardly seems like a 'red seaweed' but to a scientist it is! The red colouring is often bleached out by the sun, leaving this dark green colouring beneath it. Very common on rocks near mid-tide around the northern half of the North Island. Can be eaten but is rather chewy.

Karengo ▲

Porphyra columbina
Soon after the tide begins to go out this purplish seaweed is out of the water. Can be up to 20cm across. It is a traditional food of Māori and is often dried and packaged for sale to add to soups. Also called **parengo**.

• *Note the interrupted 'veins' or stitches*

◀ Red Ribbon Seaweed

Stenogramme interrupta
Rosy crimson to bright pink. A common delicate seaweed which is often found washed up in piles in harbours. Hold these 'ribbons' up to the light to see how the 'veins' are interrupted (broken). These vein-like stitches are found on female fronds only and are used by the seaweed to reproduce.

Seaweed / Rimurimu (Brown)

Of the three main colours of seaweed, these are dark to golden brown or olive green. Most brown seaweeds grow in slightly deeper water than the green seaweeds. But brown seaweeds still need direct sunlight to grow and don't get enough light to do well in very deep water (unless the water is exceptionally clear). Some of the longer ones with flexible stems like **bladder kelp** (*Macrocystis pyrifera*) make great skipping ropes!

Encrusting Alga
Ralfsia verrucosa
These strange wrinkled crusts on rocks and shells are a kind of seaweed. They look and feel like melted rubber. So far, no one in New Zealand has studied them in detail.

Air Cushion Weed ▲
Colpomenia sinuosa
This puffball-like seaweed grows on rocks and other seaweeds. Can be up to 10cm across. It is also known as **oyster thief** after a similar seaweed which arrived in France about 1900. There, the seaweed often grew on young oysters. As the seaweed grew and the air bladder filled, it annoyed the locals by lifting up the oysters and carrying them away! (Well, that's how the story goes; whether it's true I don't know!)

Bladder Weed ▶
Carpophyllum species
There are several kinds of brown seaweed with air-filled bladders like this. Small ones are common throughout New Zealand in rock pools at low tide; larger ones grow in deep water. The whole seaweed can be up to two metres long. But much smaller pieces like this are very often washed up.

• These beads are filled with air. When the tide comes in, these floats lift the seaweed nearer to the sunlight

Strap Weed
Xiphophora chondrophylla
Smooth and rubbery. Can be up to 50cm long. Grows thickly on steep rocks around low tide where the water surges in and out. Also known as **sword weed**.

Unless otherwise indicated, all photos are shown at life-size

• These pimply beads are filled with water which makes them good for popping and squirting

Neptune's Necklace ▶

Hormosira banksii
This is a good seaweed for squirting. Try popping the pimply olive-brown beads. Each one is filled with seawater. Can be up to 50cm long. Very common on rocks and stones around mid-tide in sheltered places. Sheep eat it, as do some people. The youngest beads at the tips taste best, but remember to collect them only from unpolluted beaches.

• Living bull kelp (not life-size)

◀ Bull Kelp / Rimurapa

Durvillaea species
Take a huge fat blade of this. Cut a section and poke the fingers of your flat palm into the pale honeycomb core of it. Like this you can make shoes, flippers, leggings, hats and so on. These blades are still used by South Island Māori for storing muttonbirds (tītī) and for cooking fish. The dried seaweed was also traditionally used for making jelly. Or use a penknife to cut a section of the stem ('holdfast') and shape it to make a mug or bouncing 'rubber' ball (as shown below). One friend even makes beautiful handcrafts out of the lacquered strands. Some blades can be 10 metres long. Very common on exposed coasts in the South Island, but also found as far north as Auckland.

• Crafts made from lacquered strands of bull kelp (not life-size)

• Rubbery ball made from bull kelp stem (see below)

• A single strand from the tip of a bull kelp frond

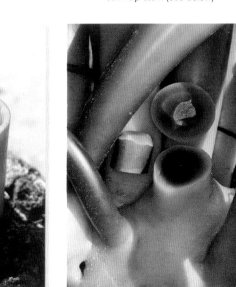

• Bull kelp stem cut and hollowed out with a penknife to make a mug (not life-size)

• Rubbery ball cut and shaped with a penknife from a short section of bull kelp stem (about half life-size)

• Here, the pale honeycomb core of the flipper can be seen

• Kelp flippers hollowed out from the thick blade of a bull kelp frond (not life-size)

27

Seaweed / Rimurimu (Green)

[Algae: Chlorophyta]

Of the three main colours of seaweeds (green, brown and red) found around New Zealand, this is the smallest group. Green seaweeds need direct sunlight to grow, so are found in shallow water only, near the high tide mark. Most of those shown here are regularly washed up onto the beach.

Green Grape Seaweed ▲
Caulerpa geminata
The bead-like leaves look like tiny grapes. Grows on rocks just below low tide around the North Island and northern South Island. Has a peppery taste and is eaten fresh in salads. Usually not much more than 10cm high. (Not so often washed up as the other seaweeds on this page.)

Gut Weed
Enteromorpha intestinalis ▲
Often forms a thick greenish carpet around sheltered rock pools near high tide and often near fresh water. In Japan, this is eaten (cooked or raw). As the common and scientific names say, it looks a bit like guts or intestines. Can grow to about 20cm long.

Sea Lettuce
Ulva lactuca
This bright green waxy seaweed is out of the water soon after the tide begins to go out. Can be up to 30cm across. Common along sheltered rocky coasts. It looks like a garden lettuce and is eaten in soups. ▼

Branching Velvet Weed ▼
Codium fragile
Has slim dark green, velvety branches. Grows on rocks just above low tide, often near sand. In Japan, it is dried, boiled and added to soup. Can be up to 30cm long.

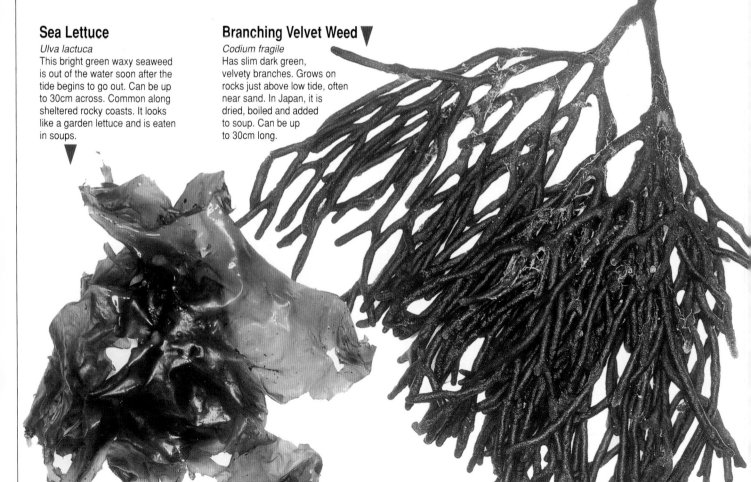

Unless otherwise indicated, all photos are shown at life-size

Plant Wash-Ups (Seeds)

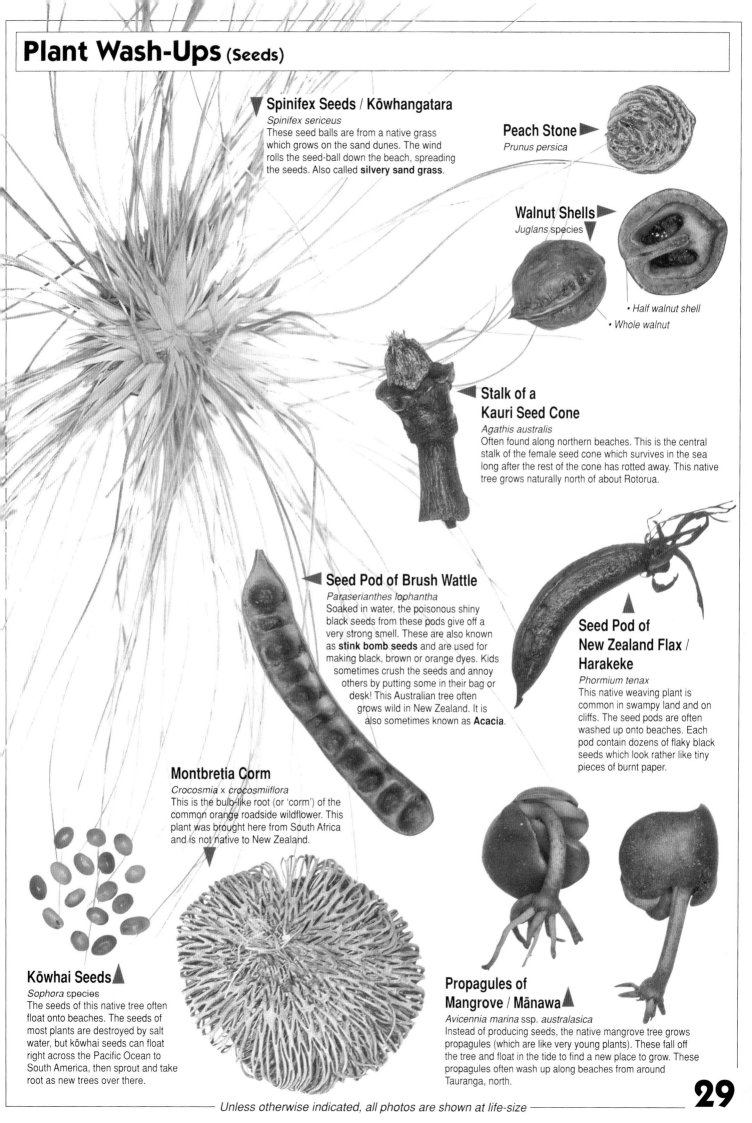

Spinifex Seeds / Kōwhangatara
Spinifex sericeus
These seed balls are from a native grass which grows on the sand dunes. The wind rolls the seed-ball down the beach, spreading the seeds. Also called **silvery sand grass**.

Peach Stone ▶
Prunus persica

Walnut Shells ▶
Juglans species

• Half walnut shell
• Whole walnut

Stalk of a Kauri Seed Cone
Agathis australis
Often found along northern beaches. This is the central stalk of the female seed cone which survives in the sea long after the rest of the cone has rotted away. This native tree grows naturally north of about Rotorua.

Seed Pod of Brush Wattle
Paraserianthes lophantha
Soaked in water, the poisonous shiny black seeds from these pods give off a very strong smell. These are also known as **stink bomb seeds** and are used for making black, brown or orange dyes. Kids sometimes crush the seeds and annoy others by putting some in their bag or desk! This Australian tree often grows wild in New Zealand. It is also sometimes known as **Acacia**.

Seed Pod of New Zealand Flax / Harakeke
Phormium tenax
This native weaving plant is common in swampy land and on cliffs. The seed pods are often washed up onto beaches. Each pod contain dozens of flaky black seeds which look rather like tiny pieces of burnt paper.

Montbretia Corm
Crocosmia x *crocosmiiflora*
This is the bulb-like root (or 'corm') of the common orange roadside wildflower. This plant was brought here from South Africa and is not native to New Zealand.

Kōwhai Seeds ▲
Sophora species
The seeds of this native tree often float onto beaches. The seeds of most plants are destroyed by salt water, but kōwhai seeds can float right across the Pacific Ocean to South America, then sprout and take root as new trees over there.

Propagules of Mangrove / Mānawa ▲
Avicennia marina ssp. *australasica*
Instead of producing seeds, the native mangrove tree grows propagules (which are like very young plants). These fall off the tree and float in the tide to find a new place to grow. These propagules often wash up along beaches from around Tauranga, north.

29

Unless otherwise indicated, all photos are shown at life-size

Plant Wash-Ups (Leaves, Gum, Lichen & Driftwood)

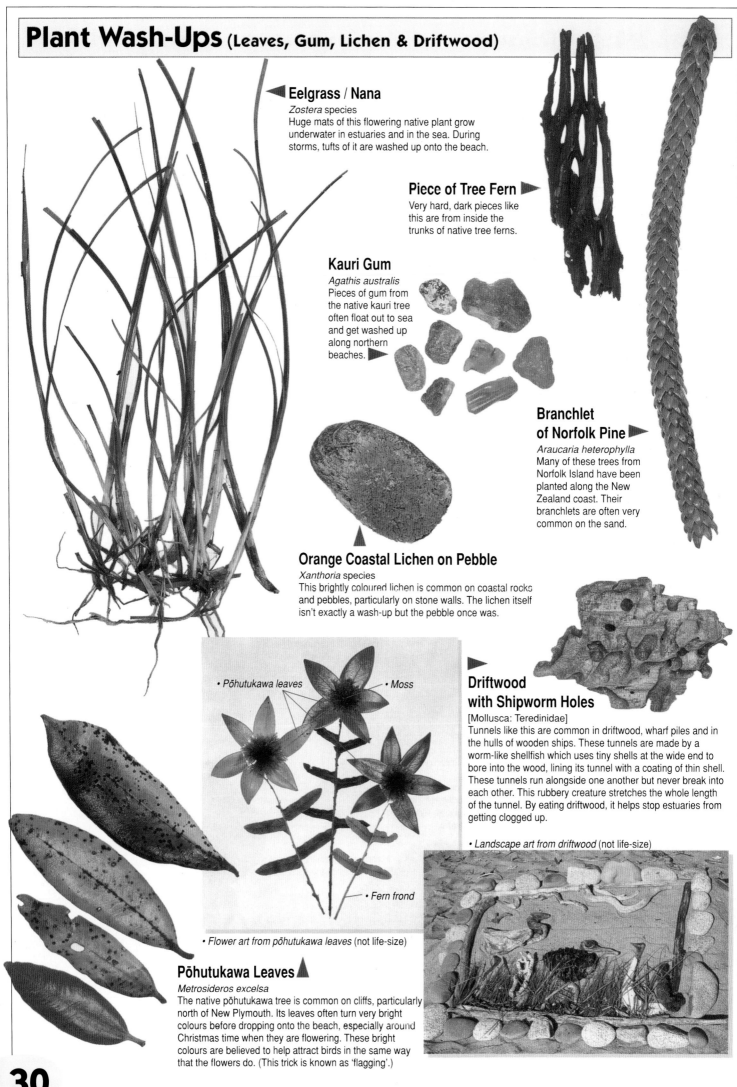

◀ Eelgrass / Nana

Zostera species
Huge mats of this flowering native plant grow underwater in estuaries and in the sea. During storms, tufts of it are washed up onto the beach.

Piece of Tree Fern ▶

Very hard, dark pieces like this are from inside the trunks of native tree ferns.

Kauri Gum

Agathis australis
Pieces of gum from the native kauri tree often float out to sea and get washed up along northern beaches. ▶

Branchlet of Norfolk Pine ▶

Araucaria heterophylla
Many of these trees from Norfolk Island have been planted along the New Zealand coast. Their branchlets are often very common on the sand.

Orange Coastal Lichen on Pebble

Xanthoria species
This brightly coloured lichen is common on coastal rocks and pebbles, particularly on stone walls. The lichen itself isn't exactly a wash-up but the pebble once was.

• *Pōhutukawa leaves*   • *Moss*

▶ Driftwood with Shipworm Holes

[Mollusca: Teredinidae]
Tunnels like this are common in driftwood, wharf piles and in the hulls of wooden ships. These tunnels are made by a worm-like shellfish which uses tiny shells at the wide end to bore into the wood, lining its tunnel with a coating of thin shell. These tunnels run alongside one another but never break into each other. This rubbery creature stretches the whole length of the tunnel. By eating driftwood, it helps stop estuaries from getting clogged up.

• *Fern frond*

• *Landscape art from driftwood* (not life-size)

• *Flower art from pōhutukawa leaves* (not life-size)

Pōhutukawa Leaves ▲

Metrosideros excelsa
The native pōhutukawa tree is common on cliffs, particularly north of New Plymouth. Its leaves often turn very bright colours before dropping onto the beach, especially around Christmas time when they are flowering. These bright colours are believed to help attract birds in the same way that the flowers do. (This trick is known as 'flagging'.)

Unless otherwise indicated, all photos are shown at life-size

Rubbish

The floating rubbish washed onto beaches tells a story. Much of it has been carried along the coast by **ocean currents**. To find out which way your local currents flow, check this map. Another easy way to find out the ocean current direction is to check whether there is a sand-spit on one side of your local river. If there is, then that will be the side the main ocean current is coming from. Similarly if the river mouth bends to one side, it will point in the direction of the passing ocean current.

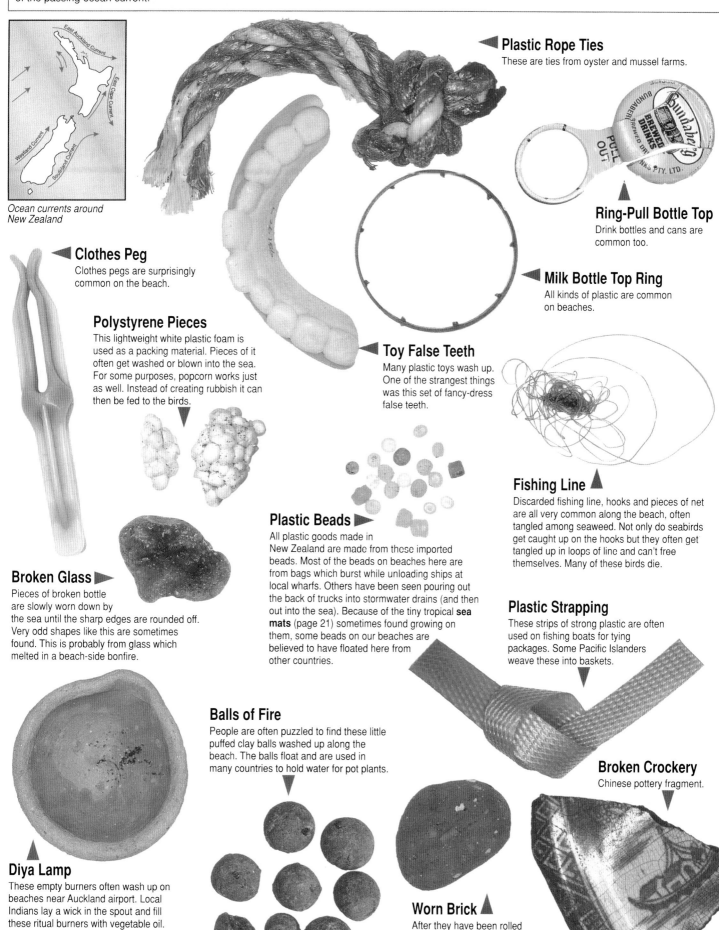

Ocean currents around New Zealand

Plastic Rope Ties
These are ties from oyster and mussel farms.

Ring-Pull Bottle Top
Drink bottles and cans are common too.

Milk Bottle Top Ring
All kinds of plastic are common on beaches.

Clothes Peg
Clothes pegs are surprisingly common on the beach.

Polystyrene Pieces
This lightweight white plastic foam is used as a packing material. Pieces of it often get washed or blown into the sea. For some purposes, popcorn works just as well. Instead of creating rubbish it can then be fed to the birds.

Toy False Teeth
Many plastic toys wash up. One of the strangest things was this set of fancy-dress false teeth.

Fishing Line
Discarded fishing line, hooks and pieces of net are all very common along the beach, often tangled among seaweed. Not only do seabirds get caught up on the hooks but they often get tangled up in loops of line and can't free themselves. Many of these birds die.

Plastic Beads
All plastic goods made in New Zealand are made from these imported beads. Most of the beads on beaches here are from bags which burst while unloading ships at local wharfs. Others have been seen pouring out the back of trucks into stormwater drains (and then out into the sea). Because of the tiny tropical **sea mats** (page 21) sometimes found growing on them, some beads on our beaches are believed to have floated here from other countries.

Broken Glass
Pieces of broken bottle are slowly worn down by the sea until the sharp edges are rounded off. Very odd shapes like this are sometimes found. This is probably from glass which melted in a beach-side bonfire.

Plastic Strapping
These strips of strong plastic are often used on fishing boats for tying packages. Some Pacific Islanders weave these into baskets.

Balls of Fire
People are often puzzled to find these little puffed clay balls washed up along the beach. The balls float and are used in many countries to hold water for pot plants.

Broken Crockery
Chinese pottery fragment.

Diya Lamp
These empty burners often wash up on beaches near Auckland airport. Local Indians lay a wick in the spout and fill these ritual burners with vegetable oil. The lamp is lit and cast afloat on the sea at funerals to symbolise the release of the dead person's soul.

Worn Brick
After they have been rolled around by the sea, pieces of brick often look like pebbles of soft brown rock.

Unless otherwise indicated, all photos are shown at life-size

Index

Where there are several page numbers, the main one is shown in **bold**.

32